KINDER . .

"I avoid sometimes the manifestations of my toughness . . . I don't have to go out and beat my chest like Tarzan . . . and assert my toughness by being brutal to people."

> —as quoted in *The New York Times,*
> March 6, 1988

GENTLER . . .

"I need combat pay for last night, I'll tell you. You know, it's Tension City when you're in there . . ."

> —commenting, the day after, on his famous interview with Dan Rather in January 1988

. . . AND ALWAYS GEORGE BUSH

"I think it might be kind of nice to have a Connecticut kid in the White House."

> —as quoted in *The New York Times,*
> March 24, 1980

WITH A LITTLE HELP FROM DAN QUAYLE

"One learns every day. Experience is a great teacher. By experience you learn. But as I enter office, I'm prepared now. Obviously, I will be more prepared as time goes on. I will know more about the office of the Presidency."

> —as quoted in *The New York Times,*
> Jan. 14, 1989

The Wit & Wisdom of
GEORGE
BUSH

With Some Reflections From Dan Quayle

Edited by
Ken Brady & Jeremy Solomon

ST. MARTIN'S PRESS/NEW YORK

THE WIT & WISDOM OF GEORGE BUSH

Copyright © 1989 by Ken Brady and Jeremy Solomon.

ISBN: 0-312-91687-6   Can. ISBN: 0-312-91688-4

Printed in the United States of America

First St. Martin's Press mass market edition / May 1989

10 9 8 7 6 5 4 3 2 1

ACKNOWLEDGMENTS

Dan Shea
Claudia Weinstein
Anna Solomon
Sharon DeLevie
Maris Strautmanis

*Dedicated to George Bush
for letting us read his lips
and to Dan Quayle
for living in this century.*

CONTENTS

The Wit & Wisdom of
GEORGE
BUSH

With Some Reflections From Dan Quayle

Experts Agree!

"George Bush is the Don Knotts of American politics."

—Peter Hart, Democratic pollster[1]

"I can read Mr. Bush's lips. I don't know if they are connected to a brain."

—Professor Robert Solow, MIT Nobel economist[2]

"He has an arms-length relationship with the English language . . . The only speech part that he has mastered completely is the non sequitur."

—Mary McGrory, *Washington Post* columnist[3]

"[He speaks] with nouns tangled by wayward verbs and clauses ambushed by preppy adverbs."

—Bernard Weinraub, *New York Times* reporter[4]

"An Ivy League cheerleader, the perfect gentleman on the way to being the perfect idiot."
                    —Murray Kempton, syndicated columnist[5]

"Boy Scout with a hormone imbalance."
                    —Kevin Phillips, Republican analyst[6]

"Reagan can portray a real macho guy. Bush can't. He comes off looking like Liberace."
                    —Texas State Senator Carl A. Parker[7]

FOOTNOTES

1. *This Week with David Brinkley,* October 1987, as quoted in *Spy,* April 1988, p. 126

2. *The MacNeil-Lehrer News Hour,* PBS, September 28, 1988

3. *Washington Post,* September 29, 1988, p. A2

4. *New York Times,* November 4, 1988, p. A18

5. *Spy,* August 1988, p. 98

6. Ibid

7. *New York Times Magazine,* Peter Applebome, October 30, 1988, p. 66

Introduction

GREAT LEADERS HAVE ALWAYS INSPIRED their followers with stirring phrases and colorful, imaginative language. Franklin Roosevelt reassured the nation with his immortal claim, "We have nothing to fear but fear itself." John F. Kennedy sought to inspire a generation with his challenge, "Ask not what your country can do for you. Ask what you can do for your country."

Our newest national leader, President George Bush, also has a way with words. However, Bush's contributions to the English language are of a far different nature. His public statements do not usually produce patriotic displays of flag-waving or misty-eyed adulation. Laughter —or a confused double-take—is a more likely result.

Bush is fast emerging as a major force on the cutting edge of topical humor. As former Reagan Chief of Staff Donald Regan reported in his recent book, one of Bush's responsibilities as Vice President was to come up with a joke or story for President Reagan every morning.[1]

But do not get the idea that George is some Kennebunkport David Letterman. Stand-up humor is not his style. Most of Bush's humorous statements pop up at the least likely moments—usually when he is trying to be dead serious.

Bush's propensity for humorous gaffes and misstatements became a running joke during the grueling 1988 campaign for the White House. Journalists and Washington, D.C., insiders have long recognized this wacky trait in him, dubbing his self-created language "Bushspeak." Newspapers routinely listed Bush's goofy slipups without comment, much as they do traffic accidents or birth and death records.

There is only one rule in Bushspeak: there are no rules. Bushspeak can be short and sweet, such as the time he said he and President Reagan "had sex."[2] Or it can be a long collection of incomplete thoughts compressed into one, tortuous sentence guaranteed to leave listeners scratching their heads.

Two subjects are almost certain to elicit a Bushspeak response: wimpiness and preppiness. With mixed and often amusing results, Bush tries valiantly to live down his image as a well-born Eastern aristocrat.

But Bushspeak proved effective on the campaign trail (George has been campaigning more or less nonstop since 1979) when nosy people actually wanted to know what positions he took on certain issues. George answered all questions straight on with such position statements as, "I'm for unions. I'm for nonunions,"[3] and "I'm for Mr. Reagan—blindly."[4] There. Any further questions?

Bush's wayward way with words became such a common topic that he even poked fun at himself, making numerous tongue-in-cheek references to his "eloquent" speaking abilities.

Fortunately for the country, President Bush is not the only one who has mastered this unusual dialect. Vice President Dan Quayle seems to be a worthy heir-apparent to Bush as the practitioner of Bushspeak. Here is a man who claims he "did not live in this century,"[5] and who explained the importance of "the bondage between parent and child."[6] The perfect number-two man. He probably considers himself just a "heartburn" away from the presidency.

George Bush has already contributed some seductively catchy phrases to the English language—read my lips; a thousand points of light; a kinder, gentler nation. However, it is likely that before long he will be better-known for some less crafted, less intentional statements. Every day he adds to the volume of Bushspeak that will be his legacy. The next time you hear him, listen closely and see if you can pick up one or two new ones.

Until then, sit back and enjoy this collection of the painfully hilarious phraseology of our new national leadership team. Study their words and enjoy a good-natured laugh or two. But be careful. With prolonged exposure, you too may begin to use phrases like "deep doo-doo."

FOOTNOTES

1. *For the Record: From Wall Street to Washington,* Donald T. Regan, Harcourt, Brace, Jovanovich (1988), p. 250

2. *New York Times,* May 5, 1988, p. A32

3. *The Washington Post,* November 3, 1984, p. 6A

4. *Spy,* August 1988, p. 100

5. *Spy,* November 1988, p. 128

6. *In These Times,* Maggie Garb, September 27, 1988, p. 5

One-Liners

CARSON AND HOPE, MOVE OVER. GROUCHO, wherever you are, you should feel proud. The torch has been passed. The new King of the One-liner is here and, best of all, he is the latest inhabitant of the Oval Office. That's right, George Bush can deliver a good, old-fashioned one-liner that, intentionally or not, leaves audiences howling with laughter.

The key word here is "intentionally." These one-liners usually develop when Bush's thoughts are a full step or two ahead of his tongue—or when they are on two completely independent paths. This generally results in an amusingly mangled statement, the bastard offspring of two unrelated ideas. Eventually, though, George realizes that he did not say what he intended. You can almost hear the skidding of tires when Bush slams on the brakes in a futile effort to salvage a coherent statement. This all-too-frequent situation leads to embarrassingly funny statements, and his desperate attempts to clarify his original statements only lead to more confusion. Or more chuckles.

A number of comedians have made a living by intentionally fracturing the English language for comic effect. Well, they might all be out of business soon as they try to compete with the Commander-in-Chief of Twisted Syntax, trying to top the one-liners of George Bush.

MR. SENSITIVITY

"Boy, they were big on crematoriums, weren't they?"—Comment during his tour of the Nazi death camp at Auschwitz, September 28, 1987[1]

"Comme çi, comme ça . . ."—While talking to a nine-year-old Hispanic student at a Harlem school[2]

"Muchissimo grazie."—At an Italian-American festival, mixing Spanish and Italian, in an attempt to say *molto grazie,* or many thanks, in Italian[3]

Introducing President Reagan to his three half-Mexican grandchildren in New Orleans, Bush referred to them as "the little brown ones over there."[4]

"I'm proud they're brown."—Defending criticism of calling his grandchildren "little brown ones.[5]

"You don't have to go to college to achieve success. We need the people who do the hard

19

physical work of our society."—Speaking to a group of Hispanic East Los Angeles high school students[6]

"These aren't animals—these are wild quail." —Responding, at the start of a four-day hunting and fishing trip, to a reporter who wanted to know how Bush's killing of "cute, cuddly animals" fit in with his goal of a kinder, gentler America[7]

DECISION 1988

"He will go down as *the* great governor of the state of California."—Praising California Governor George Deukmejian at a campaign rally September 14, 1988, in Kingsburg, California. The crowd gasped after hearing these words. In his typical enthusiasm for the task at hand, Bush had forgotten that Reagan had been governor of California.[8]

"When I'm the education President, you'll be able to send your college to children."—On the 1988 campaign trail. Later in the same speech, he referred to the high cost of college as "the high cost of courage."[9]

"The slide show is over."—Attempting to tell a 1988 campaign audience that he and Reagan had halted the nation's economic decline, that is, "the slide is over."[10]

"Narced-up terrorist kind of guys."—Announcing in October of 1988 who he would protect voters from if elected president[11]

"Today, you remember—I wonder how many Americans remember—today is Pearl Harbor Day—forty-seven years ago from this very day we were hit and hit hard at Pearl Harbor. And we were not ready."—Promoting a strong defense in a speech to the 70th Annual American Legion Convention, September 7, 1988, in Louisville, Kentucky. The Japanese attack occurred on December 7, 1941.[12]

"It used to be a kitchen in every pot."—At a campaign rally in Troy, Ohio, October 22, 1988, mangling a speech that was supposed to conclude with a criticism of Michael Dukakis' tax plan as an idea that would result in an auditor in every home[13]

"If this country . . . ever loses its interest in fishing, we got real trouble."—On the 1988 campaign trail[14]

"I have a feeling, I always have, that if you just go nasty, go ugly, it isn't an effective way to do business."—Regarding a long series of attacks on him at the 1988 Democratic convention. Bush built his campaign against Michael Dukakis around a number of negative charges and television commercials, including making an issue out the the Pledge of Allegiance, the Massachusetts prison-furlough program, and the American Civil Liberties Union.[15]

"Soon the convention will be over, and we will remember *Gone With the Wind.*"—On the unusual display of unity among Democrats at their convention[16]

"Those are two hypo-rhetorical questions."—From his debate with Michael Dukakis, September 25, 1988[17]

"These people laugh about the thousand points of life. You ought to go out and see—light. . . ."[18]

"A thousand shining hill."—An aborted attempt to invoke his famous "thousand points of light" image[19]

"I'll try to hold my charisma in check."—From his acceptance speech at the GOP convention in New Orleans in 1988[20]

"It's no exaggeration to say the undecideds could go one way or another."—Discussing the voters during the 1988 campaign[21]

A MAN OF THE WORLD

"We love your adherence to democratic principles and democratic processes."—A toast made for then-Philippine dictator Ferdinand Marcos at a 1981 inaugural ball in Manila.[22]

"I'll repeat it and stand by it . . . We should judge by the record."—Response at a news conference in Honolulu to questions about his toast to Marcos.[23]

Efforts by the Congress to cut off aid to the Nicaraguan contras "pulls the plug out from under the President of the United States."—Comment during the 1988 presidential race.[24]

"America's freedom is the example to which the world expires."—At a campaign speech in Detroit, October 1988[25]

"Hey, when the mechanics who keep those tanks running run out of work in the Soviet

Union, send them to Detroit, because we could use that kind of ability."—Reacting at a NATO meeting in Brussels to the news that none of the 350 tanks in a Soviet military maneuver had broken down[26]

"Under the very guise of the Soviet Union."—Discussing how Poland has been able to expand its freedoms[27]

"The contras are not just totalitarian—they are Marxist-Leninists. They don't believe in freedom of the press, freedom of religion."—Bush apparently meant the Nicaraguan Sandinistas. The Reagan administration was a strong supporter of the contras.[28]

"Oh boy, this brings the Afghan war close to home."—On a trip to Pakistan, looking out at an encampment of Afghan rebels.[29]

"Tell me, General, how dead is the Dead Sea?"—To Jordanian Army Chief of Staff Zeid Bin Shaker[30]

TURNING INWARD

"For seven and a half years I have worked alongside him [Ronald Reagan], and I am proud to be his partner. We have had triumphs, we have made mistakes, we have had sex . . ."
—Describing his relationship with former President Reagan at a Republican rally, May 1988, in Twin Falls, Idaho[31]

"I'm one of you."—Bush used this sentence eight times in a single speech in New Hampshire in 1988, one day after finishing third in the Iowa caucuses. Senator Robert Dole, who had finished first in Iowa, had used "I'm one of you" as his slogan there. Bush later claimed he did this as a joke.[32]

"Ah am one of y'al'."—Dressed as a cowboy in the Houston Livestock Show Parade[33]

"Texas? I'm one of them too. Can't vote in Massachusetts. Born there. I'm one of them, too."—When asked about his claim that he was a favorite son of Texas and Massachusetts as well as New Hampshire[34]

"I think it might be kind of nice to have a Connecticut kid in the White House."[35]

"In New Hampshire I said 'I am one of you.' I grew up in that part of the country. So I was armed tonight. But they wouldn't let me use my credentials—my Texas hunting license, my Texas driver's license, and my voter's registration card."—To a rally in Texas during the 1988 campaign[36]

"My heartbeat is the Texas heartbeat. . . ."[37]

"I'm legally and emotionally entitled to be what I want to be. That's what I want to be and that's what I am."—Answering questions concerning why he calls himself a Texan, despite his Eastern roots[38]

He once described his love for his sister as a "neat feeling."[39]

When informed that former President Jimmy Carter referred to him as "silly," Bush closed his lips tightly and stared ahead. He then replied, "That's what I think of that."[40]

"I'm looking introvertedly, and I don't like what I see."—After losing a 1970 election to Lloyd Bentsen for a U.S. Senate seat in Texas[41]

He remarked that voters believed he was a poor public speaker who couldn't finish a sentence without a "proposition."[42]

"I mean, like, hasn't everybody thought about becoming President for years?"—Statement made during the 1980 primary season[43]

GOLDEN OLDIES

"In array."—Describing the condition the country was in when he and President Reagan took over from Jimmy Carter in 1980[44]

In the 1984 presidential campaign during a swing through Wisconsin, Bush stopped in Green Bay and told the crowd how much he loved the Minnesota Vikings.[45]

"Nervous—nervioso, muy nervioso."—When asked how he felt the day before the key Massachusetts primary in 1980[46]

"Not with the idea of going back and killing off the fish or something, but seeing if we can't find the balance."—When asked if, as president, he would relax environmental regulations regarding auto emissions[47]

"Just a splash."—Asking for coffee at a truck stop[48]

"The idea that I got $6000 from Pat and Dick Nixon—he was a popular President then—I'd have been blowing about it."—In response to reports that Nixon gave Bush $6000 in cash for his 1970 Senate campaign and Bush never reported it[49]

"I have absolutely total confidence as to his integrity."—Commenting on Richard Nixon during the height of Watergate[50]

"If Carter can do it with no credentials, I can do it with these fantastic credentials: The fact that nobody else knows it is kind of discouraging."—Explaining why he would make a good president[51]

"Connecticut is going into its day in the sun all by itself."—Commenting, in 1980, on the upcoming Connecticut primary[52]

"I'm not doing it for that. I'm doing it because I'd do it. What's so complicated about that?"—In response to a statement that he was hanging on in a hopeless quest for the Presidency simply because his ego would not let him drop out of the race[53]

"There is something, though, that when you project income and it doesn't come in like you project, you have a revenue shortfall."—After dropping out of the 1980 presidential race amid reports of a $300,000 accounting error in his campaign that left it heavily in debt[54]

"No, not in the least. So I don't—I mean I'm here, here I am."—Explaining, in 1980, that he didn't feel like a "second choice" to run as Reagan's Vice President. A flurry of rumors had swept through the convention that Reagan was negotiating with former President Gerald Ford to join the ticket.[55]

"We're Number One, and there's a lot of idiots don't know that."—In Parsippany, New Jersey, on the general state of the country[56]

During the 1984 campaign Bush said New York Governor Mario Cuomo was like "Batman—he's everywhere," in reference to Cuomo's frequent criticisms of the Reagan administration.[57]

"The attempt to tear down our President's leadership with the knowledge of the issues has not failed."—On the effectiveness of Walter Mondale's attacks on Reagan during the 1984 campaign[58]

"That's all right. We've got another one."—Answering criticism that budget cuts had led to the resignation of James H. Webb Jr., the Secretary of the Navy.[59]

"It's the feeling of being at the end of something."—When asked what it was like to finish the 1980 presidential campaign.[60]

"Voodoo economics."—What Bush called Reagan's 1980 campaign pledge to cut taxes, raise military spending, and balance the budget at the same time. Later that year, at a debate in Baltimore after he had been chosen Reagan's running mate, Bush mumbled: "God, I wish I hadn't said that." The term continued to haunt him in the 1988 campaign, when critics, using one of Bush's expressions, referred to his economic program as "doo-doo economics."[61]

"It's the only memorable thing I've ever said, and I've regretted saying it."—On his 1980 characterization of Reagan's economic proposals as "voodoo economics"[62]

"I don't believe you can cut taxes by $70 billion and still get this budget in balance."—Before his conversion to Reaganomics[63]

FOOTNOTES

1. *Spy,* August, 1988, p. 102

2. *Wall Street Journal,* Ellen Hume, August 15, 1988, p. 40

3. *Washington Post,* Bill Peterson, July 23, 1988, p. A15

4. *Esquire,* January 1989, p. 92

5. *Spy,* November 1988, p. 124

6. *Spy,* August 1988, p. 98

7. *New York Times,* December 29, 1988

8. *New York Times,* September 15, 1988, p. B11

9. *Spy,* August 1988, p. 102

10. *New York Times,* Bernard Weinraub, November 4, 1988, p. A18

11. *Wall Street Journal,* Ronald G. Shafer, November 4, 1988, p. 1

12. *New York Times,* September 8, 1988, p. 12

13. *New York Times,* Maureen Dowd, October 22, 1988, p. L9

14. *Spy,* August 1988, p. 98

15. *Washington Post,* Bill Peterson, July 21, 1988, p. A25

16. *Washington Post,* Bill Peterson, July 22, 1988, p. A28

17. *New York Times,* September 26, 1988, p. A17

18. *Washington Post,* October 15, 1988, p. A18

19. *New York Times,* Maureen Dowd, October 12, 1988, p. A24

20. *Washington Post,* August 19, 1988, p. A28

21. *New York Times,* Bernard Weinraub, November 4, 1988, p. A18

22. The Associated Press, Lindy Washburn, July 2, 1981

23. Ibid.

24. *Spy,* August 1988, p. 99

25. *Wall Street Journal,* October 28, 1988, p. 1

26. *Wall Street Journal,* Ellen Hume, August 15, 1988, p. 40. Also, *Washington Post,* David Hoffman, December 3, 1987

27. *New York Times,* Bernard Weinraub, November 4, 1988, p. A18

28. *New York Times,* October 26, 1984, pp. C1, C2

29. *Washington Post,* Dale Rusakoff, August 20, 1984, p. A7

30. *Spy,* August 1988, p. 99

31. *New York Times,* Warren Weaver Jr. and E. J. Dionne Jr., May 12, 1988, p. A32

32. *Washington Post,* David Hoffman, February 10, 1988, p. A14

33. *Ms.,* Molly Ivins, May 1988, p. 24

34. *Washington Post,* David Hoffman, February 10, 1988, p. A14

35. *New York Times,* Richard L. Madden, March 24, 1980, p. B6

36. *Washington Post,* February 21, 1988, p. A14

37. *Washington Post,* Paul Taylor, August 5, 1988, p. A8

38. *Washington Post,* November 3, 1984, p. A6

39. *Washington Post,* July 22, 1988

40. *Washington Post,* Bill Peterson, July 22, 1988, p. A28

41. *Dallas Morning News,* November 5, 1970, p. A12

42. *New York Times,* Gerald M. Boyd, September 25, 1988

43. *Spy,* August 1988, p. 98

44. *New York Times,* Bernard Weinraub, November 4, 1988, p. A18

45. *Ms.,* Molly Ivins, May 1988, p. 24

46. *New York Times,* John Herbers, January 7, 1980, p. B8

47. *New York Times,* David E. Rosenbaum, May 16, 1980, p. B5

48. *The New Yorker,* Elizabeth Drew, October 10, 1988, p. 102

49. *New York Times,* Douglas E. Kneeland, February 19, 1980, p. A14

50. *Time,* November 21, 1988, p. 28

51. *New York Times,* from interviews with Maurice Carroll, January 5, 1980, p. 10

52. *New York Times,* Richard L. Madden, March 22, 1980, p. L7

53. *New York Times,* Douglas Kneeland, May 19, 1980, p. B13

54. *New York Times,* Douglas Kneeland, May 27, 1980, p. B9

55. *New York Times,* Douglas Kneeland, July 28, 1980, p. A16

56. *New York Times,* November 3, 1984, pp. A1, A6

57. *New York Times,* October 26, 1984, p. 8A

58. *New York Times,* October 26, 1984, pp. C1, C2

59. *Washington Post,* David Hoffman and Paul Taylor, February 29, 1988, p. A10

60. *New York Times,* A. O. Sulzberger Jr., November 4, 1980, p. B7

61. *Washington Post,* September 23, 1980

62. *President Ron's Appointment Book,* St. Martin's Press (1988), p. 27

63. *New York Times,* April 17, 1980, p. D17

TWO

A Rambling Man

TO TALK OF A TYPICAL GEORGE BUSH QUIP IS difficult—none are typical. However, there is a certain type of disjointed, rambling, hysterically funny remark that is a recognizable Bush trademark.

Bush has never heard the axiom that the shortest distance between two points is a straight line. He prefers to take the scenic route when making a point.

When he is on a roll, the Master of Bushspeak is like a manic genetic scientist—combining and recombining fragments of sentences, stray adverbs and adjectives, and two, three, or more unrelated thoughts. No one knows what strange statements will result.

So whether he is waxing poetic about the caribou in Alaska or decrying the frenzied feeding of bluefish, you know that George will take you on a blistering tour of the English language. So hold on tight. Do not bother with a map. Where you are going, it will not help.

"I'd like to see us open up that Alaska refuge, and that is important, because it was said once, remember when they built the pipeline, 'Don't build the pipeline, you get rid of the caribou.' The caribou love it. They rub up against it, and they have babies. There are more caribou in Alaska than you can shake a stick at."—Discussing the Alaskan pipeline at a GOP dinner in Nashua, New Hampshire, February 1988[1]

"But—and I—look, mental—that was a little overstated—I'd say about thirty percent."—Clarifying an earlier statement that most of the nation's homeless are mentally ill[2]

"I was shot down, and I was floating around in a little yellow raft setting a record for paddling. I thought of my family, my mom and dad, and the strength I got from them. I thought of my faith, the separation of church and state."—Relating his experiences and thoughts as a fighter pilot in World War II when he was shot down over Japanese waters; at the Old Creamery Theater, Garrison, Iowa, December 1987[3]

"I can announce that our dog is pregnant. This happened yesterday. A beautiful experience. We expect to have puppies in the White House."[4]

"Michael Dukakis speaks Spanish. I wish I did. But I have three grandchildren, my blood coursing through their veins, who are half Mexican."—Speaking about Hispanic America in an interview[5]

"I have a tendency to avoid on and on and on, eloquent pleas. I don't talk much, but I believe, maybe not articulate much, but I feel."— To reporters in New Hampshire, in February 1988, using vintage Bushspeak to explain his tendency to lapse into Bushspeak[6]

"You judge on the record . . . How does it look in a program he called 'phony,' or some one of these marvelous Boston adjectives up there about Angola?"—Attacking Dukakis in the first presidential debate, September 25, 1988[7]

"We had last night, last night we had a couple of our grandchildren with us in Kansas City— six-year-old twins, one of them went as a package of Juicy Fruit, arms sticking out of the pack, the other was Dracula. A big rally there. And Dracula's wig fell off in the middle of my speech and I got to thinking, watching those kids, and I said if I could look back and I had been President for four years: What would you like to do? Those young kids here. And I'd love to be able to say that working with our allies, working with the Soviets, I'd found a way to ban chemical and biological weapons from the face of the earth."—Discussing a 1988 Halloween night rally in Missouri[8]

"Now because of a lot of smoke and frenzying of bluefish out there, going after a drop of blood in the water, nobody knows that."—Complaining that his running mate Dan Quayle was not getting credit for being the author of the Job Training Partnership Act, *Today*, November 3, 1988[9]

"And you know, you look at the amount of people recommitting crimes with a gun—I looked up the gun registration, which I oppose. I went down—I told you or you heard me say this: But I had the guy doing up a file today."—Clarifying his position on gun control[10]

"This isn't any signal. It's a direct statement. If it's a signal, fine."—Regarding his remarks that Gerald Ford should not enter the presidential race in 1980 and that the time for a Ford presidency had passed[11]

"It doesn't have the drama of San Francisco. It doesn't have the low hemoglobin count that has blood spilling all over the floor. But our halo-blowers are as good as theirs. Our flag wavers are taller, stronger, and better."—In 1984, contrasting the Democrats' convention in San Francisco with the upcoming GOP convention[12]

"I don't know whether your history teaches you back into the early days of the Korean War and that kind of thing, but there was an old tough guy named Yakov Malik at the United Nations, and I was the U.N. ambassador then —I started dealing with the Soviets about then —1971, 1972."—History lesson delivered to Hopkinton High School in New Hampshire[13]

"If I have a tendency, and I confess to it, to avoid going on and on with great eloquent statements of belief."—Attempting to explain Bushspeak[14]

"Some of them are going after me because my mom and dad could look after me when we were born. I had nothing to do with that. When I ran for office in Texas they said this guy's from New England. I said, wait a minute, I couldn't help that, I wanted to be near my mother at the time."—In response to a question at an "Ask George Bush" forum that he represented the Eastern establishment wing of the Republican party[15]

"And you've got to be careful here because there's a safety factor, but I think these things —and then I am also one who believes we've got to go the extra mile in clean—being sure that that blood supply is pure."—During his September 25, 1988, debate with Dukakis, in response to a question concerning AIDS and speeding up the process for releasing new drugs that show potential for treating the disease[16]

"We are going to make some changes and some tough choices before we go to deployment on the Midgetman missile or on the Minuteman, whatever it is. We're going to have to— the MX—we're going to have to do that. It's Christmas. Wouldn't it be nice to be perfect? Wouldn't it be nice to be the iceman so you never make mistakes? These are the—these are the—these are the—my answer is do not make these unilateral cuts."—September 25, 1988, in Bush's first debate with Michael Dukakis. The "iceman" referred to Dukakis's reputation of being cold and machinelike. The Christmas line was a gibe at Bush's own famous remarks that Pearl Harbor Day was on September 7 instead of December 7[17]

While reciting the Pledge of Allegiance at a Flag City, U.S.A. celebration in Findlay, Ohio, Bush said "liberty" instead of "republic," "freedom and justice" instead of "liberty and justice" and omitted the word "indivisible" from the pledge. An aide said later that Bush had rendered an interpretation of the pledge. During the 1988 campaign Bush harshly criticized Governor Michael Dukakis for not signing a Massachusetts bill that would have required schoolchildren to start the day with the Pledge of Allegiance.[18]

"It taught me something I've known, but it brought it home. You can get into a combative high-tension situation and still do what the Vikings may have to do more than they like. Hold out your hand, shake hands and go about your business, and that's what politics ought to be and I give her credit for that."—On a campaign stop in Green Bay, Wisconsin, intending to refer to the Green Bay Packers instead of the rival Minnesota Vikings[19]

"I'll tell you what I was thinking of. I flew a combat mission. My last one was over Manila. And he [Ferdinand Marcos] was down there fighting imperialism . . . And he had just lifted martial law, and he had just called for new elections, and all of those things happened because the Philippines do crave democracy . . . And if he is corrupt, out he goes."—From his debate with Michael Dukakis, September 25, 1988[20]

During a June 1988 appearance on ABC's *Nightline,* Bush repeatedly called host Ted Koppel "Dan," apparently confusing him with Dan Rather. During a commercial, a Bush staffer taped a hastily-made sign to Bush's monitor that said "Ted."[21]

FOOTNOTES

1. *Wall Street Journal,* Ellen Hume, August 15, 1988, p. 40

2. *Washington Post,* Mary McGrory, September 29, 1988, p. A2

3. *Wall Street Journal,* Ellen Hume, August 15, 1988, p. 40

4. *New York Times,* January 4, 1988, p. 7

5. *USA Today,* July 28, 1988

6. *Washington Post,* Mary McGrory, September 29, 1988, p. A2

7. *Spotlight,* October 1988, p. 50

8. *Boston Globe,* Curtis Wilkie, November 3, 1988, p. 28

9. *New York Times,* Bernard Weinraub, November 4, 1988, p. A18

10. *New York Times,* from interviews with Maurice Carroll, January 5, 1980, p. 10

11. *New York Times,* March 10, 1980, p. B10

12. *Washington Post,* August 21, 1984, p. A9

13. *Washington Post,* February 12, 1988, p. A18

14. Ibid.

15. *Washington Post,* David Hoffman, February 16, 1988, p. A6

16. *New York Times,* September 26, 1988, p. A17

17. Ibid.

18. *New York Times,* September 17, 1988

19. *Washington Post,* Myra MacPherson, October 26, 1984, p. C1

20. *New York Times,* September 26, 1988, p. A17

21. *Esquire,* January 1989, p. 92. Also *Spy,* November 1988

THREE

I Am *Not* a Wimp!

PERHAPS THE MOST ANNOYING CRITICISM that has been leveled at Bush is that he is a weak man, a "wimp," chosen to be Reagan's Vice President because of his accommodating nature. Plagued by his wimp image, Bush will lash out at critics with a startling ferocity. This hyper-aggressiveness is meant to show what a macho man George really is, but instead it usually only embarrasses his followers and reinforces his whiny reputation.

George has been known to pick verbal fights with television anchorpersons. He goes out of his way to talk about sports and how athletic he is—painfully out of the way. He spices his language with tough, locker-room style words, explaining that he learned them while competing in Texas athletics. And he always brings up Texas —cowboys and oil wells and all that manly stuff.

Yet, in reality, George Bush seldom appears comfortable bragging about how tough he is. It seems forced. It also sends a mixed message when one day he talks about a "kinder, gentler nation" and the next day he imitates Clint Eastwood.

But we should not be too critical. Otherwise, George is liable to hunt us down and "kick a little ass."

"I need combat pay for last night, I'll tell you. You know, it's Tension City when you're in there." And later the same day he added, "The bastard didn't lay a glove on me . . . that guy makes Leslie Stahl look like a pussy."—Commenting, the day after, on his famous interview with CBS news anchor Dan Rather in January 1988[1]

During the vice presidential debate with Geraldine Ferraro, Bush accused Walter Mondale of saying the U.S. Marines in Lebanon had died in shame. Mondale, who had actually said the United States had been humiliated in Lebanon, strenuously denied Bush's accusation. After Bush refused to retract his remark, Mondale said, "George Bush doesn't have the manhood to apologize." Asked to respond to Mondale's challenge, Bush replied, "I'll lay my record on manhood against Mondale's any time."[2]

"Big guy, six-four, tough. One time when I was less than truthful he picked up a—I don't know whether it was a squash racket, or a— looked like a big stick."—Recalling how his father would discipline him[3]

"Those bastards in the press."—Discussing the press with a supporter in the locker room of a Detroit health club in October 1988[4]

"I wrote the best anti-terrorism report written."—Macho defense of his role as chairman of Reagan's Task Force on Combating Terrorism, made in the first presidential debate with Dukakis, October 25, 1988[5]

"I avoid sometimes the manifestations of my toughness . . . I don't have to go out and beat my chest like Tarzan . . . and assert toughness by being brutal to people."[6]

"We tried to kick a little ass last night." Remarking on his 1984 vice presidential debate with Geraldine Ferraro. When he realized that a television microphone was picking up his words, Bush exclaimed, "Whoops! Oh, God, he heard me! Turn that thing off!" A few days later, perhaps in a show of solidarity for her husband, Bush's wife Barbara decided to join the fun by telling reporters that Ferraro was a "four-million dollar—I can't say it, but it rhymes with rich." She later claimed she meant to imply that Ferraro was a "witch." Bush's press secretary Peter Teeley also had described Ferraro as "bitchy."[7]

When television interviewer George Sells of WJBK-TV asked Bush if he approved of his staff passing out buttons that read KICK ASS, GEORGE! Bush replied that he "doesn't have any control over that staff, it appears. I wish I did at times."—Basking in the afterglow of his "kick ass" comment[8]

"Anybody who's ever been involved in athletics—particularly Texas athletics—knows what I said. . . . It was a way of expressing victory."—Explaining his "kick ass" remark[9]

"I need a hot dog and I desperately need a beer."—At a beer and hot dog rally. The hot dogs and beer had run out forty-five minutes earlier[10]

"You're talking to an old Navy pilot, where we used to fly wing to wing, the guys' wingtips almost touching. Two hundred feet? That seems like a mile to me."—Unconcerned that a small, unauthorized plane had come within 200 feet of Air Force Two[11]

He referred to a reporter who inquired about the status of his then-unreleased tax information as "some little guy at a press conference." Bush was annoyed that the reporter asked him about "wrongdoing" associated with his taxes.[12]

"You learn that the rodeo is full of hard encounters with the ground. And you learn to pick yourself up and dust yourself off and get back on the horse again."—Relating a cowboy analogy to a Texas crowd. Previously on the same swing, Bush had visited the National Cowboy Hall of Fame, hung around with former Dallas Cowboys quarterback Roger Staubach, attended a barbecue at a ranch near San Antonio, and rode behind the Texas A&M marching band at the annual Houston Livestock Show and Rodeo Parade.[13]

"Lived in a shotgun house with a bedroom and a small kitchen. Shared a bathroom with two local women who were very nice and very friendly. Turned out they were even friendlier than we knew. We found out that our address was well-known throughout the town, lots of fellows knew it by heart."—On living in Odessa, Texas, in 1948[14]

"We've had [tennis star] Ivan Lendl here at the house. But we never got the press over and said, 'Hey, Lendl is coming here because I'm the great athletic aficionado.' But now I'd probably do that."[15]

"Jimmy Dean will be here next week. Loretta Lynn starts every concert saying 'I'm for

George Bush.' "—Reaffirming his country and western connections[16]

"Go look at my radio. 98.7 WMZQ."—Referring to a country and western station, proving that he really does like C&W music[17]

In a *USA Today* article Bush was asked if his public image matched reality. Bush said, "Much different. For example, I like pork rinds. But that doesn't fit the mold."[18]

During an August 1988 interview with CBS News anchor Dan Rather, Bush patted his wife's bottom.[19]

"I like 'em all. I like exercise. I think maybe fishing is my favorite. But then there's tennis."
—Explaining his manly love of athletics and the outdoors[20]

"They [the Democrats] were the fumble and we are the recovery."—Stretching a football analogy to the limit, at a rally in Jackson, Tennessee, on September 26, 1988[21]

"If this doesn't work out, I'm gonna be the pissedest-off guy around."—To a reporter at the

1980 Republican convention in Detroit on his desire to be named to the number-two spot on the ticket[22]

FOOTNOTES

1. *Washington Post,* January 26, 1988, p. 1A, and January 27, 1988

2. *Ms.,* Magazine, Molly Ivins, May 1988, p. 24

3. From an interview with David Frost. *New York Times,* Bernard Weinraub, October 11, 1988, p. A29

4. *Newsday,* D. D. Guttenplan and Ken Fireman, October 27, 1988, p. 5

5. *Spotlight,* October 1988, p. 50

6. *New York Times,* Randall Rothenburg, March 6, 1988, p. 48

7. *New York Times,* October 13, 1984, p. A6

8. *Washington Post,* October 25, 1984

9. *Washington Post,* October 14, 1984, p. A6

10. *New York Times,* March 7, 1980, p. D15

11. *Washington Post,* John Mintz, October 20, 1984

12. *Washington Post,* September 30, 1984, p. A14

13. *Washington Post,* February 21, 1988, p. A14

14. *Washington Post,* July 18, 1988, p. A21

15. Ibid

16. Ibid

17. *Washington Post,* Scott Patton, August 2, 1988, p. E7

18. *Esquire,* January 1989, p. 93

19. *Spy,* November 1988, pp. 124, 126

20. *New York Times,* January 2, 1989, p. 11

21. *The New Yorker,* Elizabeth Drew, October 10, 1988, p. 111

22. *Spy,* August 1988, p. 99

FOUR

No Beating Around
the Bush

LIKE MANY SUCCESSFUL POLITICIANS, George Bush is often criticized for not taking stands on issues. But perhaps more than most politicians, he has been accused of being little more than an ambitious functionary. His harshest critics go so far as to say he lacks any strong beliefs of his own. Of course, Bush strenuously denies this, and he points to the numerous statements he has made concerning his personal and political convictions.

Some of this criticism is related to Bush's exuberant personality. As Vice President for eight years, it was his job to promote the policies of the administration, and George took to this job with relish. He was so ecstatic in portraying the benefits of the Reagan Revolution that he was widely ridiculed as Reagan's cheerleader. George had to endure more than his share of pom-pom jokes and harsh political cartoons.

His other problem is that he is not an idealogue. Unlike Ronald Reagan or Barry Goldwater, Bush is not driven by a vision of how to shape the world. He has always seen himself as a public servant and a team player.

So, since no one else ever does it, let us take a minute to examine exactly where our President stands on the issues.

"I hope I stand for anti-bigotry, anti-Semitism, anti-racism. That is what drives me. That is one thing I feel very, very strongly about." Expressing his opposition to discrimination, at a campaign rally in Columbus, Ohio, September 1988. Later that day he told another Ohio audience that he did not want the country to return to the bad economic times and high interest rates that existed "ten days before I was sworn in as President of the United States." He meant to say Vice President[1]

". . . make sure that everybody who has a job wants a job." Announcing the top goal of his presidency[2]

"I'm for Mr. Reagan—blindly."—As Vice President, responding to questions about his own views on the issues[3]

"I am not your basic intellectual."—Self-analysis made during an interview with *New York Times Magazine* editor Randall Rothenburg[4]

"I've brought my brains along, let's listen to him."—Introducing his aide in National Security Council meetings in 1975 when Bush was chief of the CIA[5]

"Inarticulate as though I may be."—Boasting to reporters during the 1988 campaign that he controls the content of his speeches[6]

"I kind of think I'm a scintillating kind of fellow. I think I'm a charismatic son of a gun."—Speaking to reporters in May 1988[7]

"But how many people that pause to find themselves wondering who they were, uncertain of themselves, have the blessings that come from strength of family?"—Self-reflection with Randall Rothenburg of the *New York Times Magazine*[8]

"Because then all these people who want to know who I am, what I believe—all these [journalists] of the world, who want me to stretch out and satisfy their psychoanalytical desires—I'll say, here's who I am. I've been telling you that for twenty years, or forty, I've been living who I am—and now you know."—Clearing up once and for all that identity thing[9]

"We can now break the back of inflation, and we can increase employment. We are pessimistic."—Enthusiastically explaining his economic program during a GOP debate in New Hampshire in 1980[10]

"Do I favor mandatory crimes for people who are creating a crime with a gun? Yes—I mean mandatory sentencing."—Outlining his "get tough" approach to crime[11]

"I believe in unions. I believe in nonunions." —Responding to a question about his views on organized labor while touring a nonunion furniture factory in North Carolina[12]

At the Republican convention in 1984 he described himself as "a conservative but . . . not a nut about it."[13]

"Excellent! Strong! Exciting!"—Commenting on Ronald Reagan's positions in 1980, including a GOP platform that opposed the Equal Rights Amendment and called for a constitutional amendment banning abortion. During the 1980 primary campaign Bush had supported the ERA and had opposed the abortion amendment.[14]

"Nobody has to say it's a tremendous 100,000 percent success."—Defending Reagan's Mideast policy and commenting on the terrorist car bomb that killed more than 250 Marines in Beirut[15]

"Aid for [Families with] Dependent Children is up. Spending for food stamps is way, way up under the Reagan administration. AFDC is up under the Reagan administration. And I am not going to be found wrong on that, I am sure of my facts."—During his debate with Geraldine Ferraro on October 11, 1984. Office of Management and Budget figures in fiscal 1984 show that the federal government spent $11.8 billion on food stamps. Adjusted for inflation that represented a 9 percent cut from 1981. OMB figures also show that changes implemented by the Reagan administration reduced AFDC benefits by 21 percent when compared with 1981.[16]

"Do you know what wins elections? It's who puts money into this and who takes money out."—As he pulled out his billfold and pounded it on the podium at a 1984 Republican rally[17]

"I just have to be vague about the answer, but I certainly emphathize with the problem."—In answer to a question in Iowa about the politically sensitive "notch-baby" problem, in which people born between 1917 and 1921 are denied full Social Security benefits[18]

"I want to be the education President."—After seven years of being part of an administration that reduced Department of Education funding by $1.7 billion[19]

"The general support for the whole concept of educational excellence. It wasn't individual policy-oriented. You heard the President speak out on things, and be an executive Vice President, but I can't say I identify with any specific educational goal."—When asked what he had done for education during his seven years as Vice President and what specifically he would do to make himself the "education president"[20]

"I won't take a view. There will be two views."—On a controversy involving the Soviet Backfire bomber during Bush's tenure as CIA chief in 1976. Defense experts were split vehemently on whether the bomber should be considered an intercontinental strategic weapon or whether its usefulness was limited to Europe and Asia. Not wanting to alienate anyone, Bush sent a report to the White House containing both views. It is typical to include more than one view in such a report, but it is unusual for the CIA not to take a position.[21]

"Now I'm having trouble with these questions because they are putting me beyond where I want to be, and so if I don't answer some of them from here on in, it's because I am focusing on November eighth, and I don't want to be dragged beyond that because things seem to be going well now."—Explaining why he did not want to answer reporters' questions concerning where he would cut spending, how he would handle Nicaragua, and whom he would consider for his cabinet[22]

At a press conference on November 7, 1980, featuring the just-elected Reagan and Bush, a reporter noted that conservative elements of the party would be watching Bush, who had been perceived as a liberal Republican during the primary campaign, to make sure that he stuck to the party line. Reagan said, "I'll let George speak for himself, and I'll speak for myself."After a brief comment, Reagan asked Bush if he cared to comment, and Bush declined without saying a word.[23]

"That's why I'll be a great conservative and environmental President. I plan to fish and hunt as much as I can."[24]

"I'm going to be so much better a President for having been at the CIA that you're not going to believe it."—During the 1980 primary season[25]

While criticizing Michael Dukakis on pollution in Boston Harbor, Bush held up a crab to demonstrate the threat to sea life. The crab promptly bit him.[26]

57

"[An] honorable man."—How he described Frederic Malek, deputy chair of the Republican National Committee, after Malek was forced to resign over a news report that he had compiled a list of Jews at the Bureau of Labor Statistics[27]

"There are three people on our ticket that are knowledgeable in the race, knowledgeable in defense, and Dan Quayle is one of them."—In the September 25, 1988, debate with Dukakis, apparently meaning to say there were three people in the race who understood defense issues—Senator Lloyd Bentsen, Quayle, and himself[28]

"Yeah, I think there's some social changes going on . . . AIDS, for example, uh, is a, is a, uh, disease for, disease of poverty in a sense. It's where the hopelessness is. It's bigger than that of course."—In reply to a question about why people use drugs[29]

"The question is, how many relatives does he have in Iowa? That's the only thing I want to know."—After having his picture taken with Lech Walesa in Warsaw, referring to the upcoming Iowa caucuses[30]

"To hear these guys wringing their hands about everything being wrong with this country, I'm sorry. I just am all depressed, want to switch over to see *Jake and the Fatman* on CBS."—Statement made during a debate on NBC in December 1987[31]

"We cannot gamble with inexperience in that Oval Office."—Said to a rally September 26, 1988, in Jackson, Tennessee, with his forty-one-year-old running mate Dan Quayle standing next to him[32]

FOOTNOTES

1. The Madison, Wisconsin, *Capital Times,* September 17, 1988, p. 3

2. *Wall Street Journal,* Ronald G. Shafer, September 18, 1988, p. 1

3. *Spy,* August 1988, p. 100

4. *New York Times Magazine,* March 6, 1988, p. 29

5. *New York Times Magazine,* Randall Rothenburg, March 6, 1988, p. 46

6. *New York Times,* Bernard Weinraub, November 4, 1988, p. A18

7. *Time,* May 9, 1988, p. 38

8. *New York Times Magazine,* Randall Rothenburg, March 6, 1988, p. 61

9. *Life,* Brock Brower, May 1988, p. 140

10. *New York Times,* February 21, 1980, p. B12

11. *New York Times,* January 5, 1980, p. 10

12. *Washington Post,* November 3, 1984, p. A6

13. *Washington Post,* November 3, 1984, pp. A1, A6

14. *Washington Post,* October 26, 1984, pp. C1, C2

15. *Washington Post,* October 17, 1984, p. A4

16. *Washington Post,* October 12, 1984, p. A16

17. *Washington Post,* September 26, 1984, p. A14

18. *Washington Post,* January 24, 1988, p. A11

19. *Esquire,* January 1989, p. 93

20. *Washington Post,* February 28, 1988, p. A9

21. *Washington Post,* August 10, 1988, p. A1

22. *Washington Post,* October 17, 1988, p. A1

23. *New York Times,* November 7, 1980, p. A15

24. *New York Times,* January 2, 1989, p. 11

25. *Spy,* August 1988, p. 98

26. *The New Yorker,* Elizabeth Drew, October 10, 1988, p. 101

27. *The New Yorker,* Elizabeth Drew, October 10, 1988, p. 100

28. *New York Times,* September 26, 1988, p. A17

29. *In These Times,* June 22–July 5, 1988

30. *Spy,* August 1988, p. 99

31. *Spy,* August 1988, p. 101

32. *The New Yorker,* Elizabeth Drew, October 10, 1988, p. 111

FIVE

Poppy the Preppy Humorist

UNLIKE RECENT PRESIDENTS, GEORGE HERbert Walker Bush is a true blue-blood. Raised in the affluent New York City bedroom community of Greenwich, Connecticut, both his father and grandfather were New York City investment bankers. George, or "Poppy," as he was nicknamed, graduated from Phillips Academy prep school and Yale. Though he has tried hard to portray himself as a regular guy—for example, by professing a love for pork rinds, beer, and country music—he hasn't been able to shake his preppy image.

Again, these humorous statements are almost always unintentional, usually made when Bush's guard is down. In a relaxed moment he may mention playing squash, coming-out parties, or he might simply drop a foreign phrase at an inappropriate moment.

Often the funniest part about these Bushisms is that George does not even get his own joke. To him, it is the most natural thing in the world to talk about being given a "boy" to play tennis with him.

Do not worry, George. We will explain the jokes to

you. Just keep them coming. We will even spring for the pork rinds. With just a splash of Tabasco, please.

"He would have been in deep doo-doo."—In 1986 when asked what would happen to a Chinese official who became too friendly with Americans[1]

"A lot of people who support me were at an air show, they were off at their daughter's coming-out party, they were teeing up at the golf course in that all-important last round, and they were turning out at high school reunions." —Analyzing why he lost an Ames, Iowa, GOP straw poll, October 14, 1987[2]

"Oh, yes. They gave me a boy to play tennis with."—When asked, after returning from China in 1975, whether he had met any of the Chinese people[3]

"[I've been] catching the dickens from friends."—Referring to the Reagan administration's arms-for-hostages deal with Iran[4]

"Fini!"—At a 1988 campaign rally in Cedar Rapids, Iowa, after being accused of supporting abortion by a teenage girl in the audience, Bush walked up to the girl, grabbed a flier for presidential candidate Jack Kemp out of her hands, and shouted this at her as he ripped the flier into pieces[5]

"Ah, yes, the arms control lass."—Referring to a *Time* magazine reporter who had interviewed him on foreign policy[6]

"Come for burgers and bloodies with the Bushes."—Printed invitation to a 1988 campaign fund-raiser in New Hampshire[7]

"I don't disappear when you mention it. I would have a few years ago."—Concerning his membership in the Yale secret society Skull and Bones[8]

"Hey, for months I sat around and listened to that character calling me Ronald Reagan in a J. Press suit."—Explaining why he had begun to lash out at presidential candidate John B. Anderson[9]

"Tough as horseradish."—Describing the Soviets and their approach to arms negotiations[10]

"I mean, whine on harvest moon."—During his debate with Geraldine Ferraro in October 1984, in response to criticisms from the Mondale-Ferraro camp[11]

"You know how it is being married to a WASP woman."—Explaining that wife Barbara made him wear his preppy striped watchband to an Italian-

American banquet, though he had initially objected to wearing it[12]

"Absolutely not. There's no difference between me and the President on taxes. No more nitpicking. Zippity dooh-dah. Now it's off to the races."—A remark after a speech in Denver, in response to questions that he and Reagan held different views on a tax cut[13]

Bush claimed Michael Dukakis's foreign policy beliefs were ". . . born in Harvard Yard's boutique."[14]

"Things are boiling here. Wow!"—A note to Richard Nixon's secretary Rose Mary Woods, while Bush was ambassador to the United Nations, regarding the controversy over seating China at the U.N.[15]

"Do I have a mounting confidence that I could lead? You bet. Would I be a good President? . . . I'd be a crackerjack!"—Statement during the 1980 primary season[16]

"Gee, what good people Reagan has around him. These guys are really bright. Really bright. . . . Gosh, a new President can really make a difference!"—During the 1980 Republican convention, spoken before Ronald Reagan had chosen a vice presidential running mate, a position Bush openly coveted[17]

"Look, we've got twenty-four hours, and by gosh we're going to do this thing with a certain feeling and a certain style and then we'll figure out what to do."—To one of his sons at the GOP convention in 1980, reacting to rumors that Reagan would choose Gerald Ford as a running mate instead of Bush[18]

"Me? Oh, please. I don't think so."—After an especially vibrant speech, in reply to a question about him becoming the "tough guy" on the GOP ticket while Ronald Reagan remained above the bickering[19]

FOOTNOTES

1. *Wall Street Journal,* Ellen Hume, August 15, 1988, p. 40

2. Ibid

3. Ibid

4. *Spy,* August 1988, p. 100

5. *Ms.,* May 1988, p. 24. Also *Esquire,* January 1989, p. 93

6. *Washington Post,* September 27, 1988, p. A2

7. *Ms.,* Molly Ivins, May 1988, p. 24

8. *New York Times,* Douglas Kneeland, March 7, 1980, p. D15

9. *New York Times,* Richard L. Madden, March 25, 1980, p. B8

10. *Washington Post,* November 3, 1984, p. 6A

11. *Washington Post,* October 12, 1984, p. A16

12. *Washington Post,* September 17, 1984, p. A7

13. *Washington Post,* Dale Rusakoff, August 9, 1984, p. A7

14. *Washington Post,* July 18, 1988, p. A17

15. *Washington Post,* August 9, 1988, p. A8

16. *Spy,* August 1988, p. 98

17. *Spy,* August 1988, p. 99

18. *New York Times,* Douglas E. Kneeland, November 6, 1980, p. A25

19. *Washington Post,* September 5, 1984, p. A7

SIX

"Out of the Loop"

GEORGE BUSH'S INVOLVEMENT WITH THE events that came to be known as the Iran-contra affair provided Americans with a new catch phrase, "out of the loop."

As Vice President, Bush insisted repeatedly that he was "out of the loop" on the Reagan administration's arms deal with Iran and the illegal contra supply operation. Yet evidence indicates the truth to be otherwise. As Bob Woodward and Walter Pincus of the *Washington Post* have written:

> Vice President Bush watched the secret arms sale to Iran unfold step by step and was more informed of details than he has acknowledged, because of his regular attendance at President Reagan's morning national security briefings, and other meetings, according to his statements to the Tower commission, other Iran-contra documents,

and interviews with former administration officials.[1]

Like President Reagan, Bush found himself in a precarious position. If he knew about the arms-for-hostages swap, then he would have to explain why he endorsed such a controversial and ill-fated plan. If he did not know, then he cast doubt on whether he played a significant role in the Reagan administration.

But Bush managed to walk this tightrope successfully.

For a time it appeared the Iran-contra affair would become a major issue in the presidential election of 1988. Early in the year the major newspapers and television networks covered it extensively, and some of Bush's rivals—both Democratic and Republican—tried to use it to damage Bush at the polls.

However, the story never caught the public's fancy. As memories of Oliver North's television testimony faded, the voters turned their attention to other issues, such as the Pledge of Allegiance, the Massachusetts prison-furlough program, and Dan Quayle's college grade-point average.

This chapter explores the numerous, often embarassingly amusing, prevarications Bush has used to define and redefine his role in the Byzantine affair.

"If you would look at page 502 of the congressional report, you will see that the report clears me completely."—Standard response to questions about his role in the Iran-contra affair. Page 502 of the congressional Iran-contra report is from the dissenting minority of the congressional panel. Signed by eight loyal Republicans, this dissent to the majority report was called "pathetic" by another GOP lawmaker on the panel[2]

"I know a lot—close to it—but I don't know whether I knew everything."—On whether he knew as much about the deal as President Reagan did[3]

In the now-famous interview with CBS anchor Dan Rather on January 25, 1988, Bush said he first learned of the arms-for-hostages deal in December 1988, when Senator David Durenberger briefed him on the affair. In the same interview, however, he said he only "went along with" the trade because he wanted to rescue William Buckley, CIA Beirut station chief, who had been taken captive and tortured by his captors.

Contradictory as they are, neither claim holds much truth. The arms-for-hostages story had broken in the national press in early November 1986, a month before he said he was briefed by Senator Durenberger. As for Buckley, according to the Tower report, the United States had reliable information in October 1985, that Buckley was already dead.

"If I'd have sat there and heard Secretary George Shultz express [opposition] strongly, maybe I would have had a stronger view."— According to the findings of the Congressional Iran-contra report Secretary of State George Shultz strenuously opposed the covert Iran-contra operation.[4]

"I'm in on everything. If our policies aren't working, I can't say, 'wait a minute, I'm not to blame' . . . I feel I'm a full partner."[5]

"No, I did not . . . No, not at that juncture, certainly it wasn't clear."—Responding to a question about whether he was aware of the arms-for-hostages swap in January of 1986. House and Senate committees investigating the incident indicated that the nature of the deal was clear in White House conversations at the time[6]

Bush said he expressed "reservations" about the plan, and National Security Adviser Admiral John Poindexter had testified about these reservations. Poindexter's description of Bush's position was classified "top secret" by the White House[7]

"I'm not a kiss-and-teller."—In response to questions about what he knew about the affair[8]

"Time's up."—During a televised debate on NBC with presidential candidate Alexander Haig, when Haig pressed him for details of his involvement in the Iran-contra affair[9]

". . . I don't think it's fair to judge a whole career, it's not fair to judge my whole career by a rehash on Iran. How would you like it if I judged your career by those seven minutes when you walked off the set in New York? Would you like that?"—From his heated interview with Dan Rather on the *CBS Evening News,* referring to an incident when Rather stormed off the set because he thought the broadcast of the U.S. Open tennis match would run into his evening newscast. The incident resulted in the network going to black for seven minutes, a major embarrassment for Rather and CBS[10]

"There is no one on the Vice President's staff who is directing or coordinating an operation in Central America."—Said in response to the downing of a cargo plane containing Eugene Hasenfus over Nicaragua just before the Iran-contra affair broke. House and Senate investigations showed that Felix Rodriguez, who was involved in the secret airlift, had been placed there by the office of the Vice President[11]

FOOTNOTES

1. *Washington Post,* January 7, 1988

2. *Ms.,* Molly Ivins, May 1988, p. 25

3. *Washington Post,* January 8, 1988, p. A6

4. *In These Times,* Jeff Nason and Malcolm Byrne, February 16, 1988, p. 3

5. Interview with Richard Fly, *Business Week,* August 18, 1988

6. *Washington Post,* January 6, 1988, p. A6

7. Ibid

8. *Washington Post,* David Hoffman, January 7, 1988, p. A1

9. *Washington Post,* January 7, 1988, p. A6

10. *Washington Post,* David Hoffman, January 26, 1988, p. A1

11. *Washington Post,* David Hoffman, August 12, 1988, p. A10

SEVEN

That "Thing" Thing

ALTHOUGH SHAKESPEARE ONCE WROTE, "The Play's the Thing," George Bush might disagree. George might paraphrase the Bard by saying, "The thing's the thing."

That is because Bush has this thing about using the word "thing." He employs it as a crutch when he cannot quite come up with the right word. Or even the wrong word. Or any word at all.

This unique aspect of Bushspeak, his impulsive, embarrassingly inarticulate statements using the word "thing," can only be called his "thing" thing.

"Did you come here and say, 'The heck with it, I don't need this darn thing?' Did you go through that withdrawal thing?"—To a recovering drug addict at a Newark, N.J., drug clinic[1]

"Oh, the vision thing."—Response to a friend's suggestion that he spend a few days alone to think about what he proposed to do as President[2]

"Your dedication and tireless work with the hostage thing."—Handwritten note to Oliver North praising his efforts to release American hostages in Lebanon[3]

"Boy, I'm glad that thing is over! I don't need any more of that."—After the 1984 vice presidential debate with Geraldine Ferraro[4]

"I haven't selected her. But let me tell you, this gender thing is history. You're looking at a guy who sat down with Margaret Thatcher across the table and talked about serious issues."—Responding to questions about who his running mate would be in the 1988 campaign[5]

". . . but look at the pressure now on this inflation thing."[6]

"The whole ethnic thing in our country, the pride we take in where we came from and what we are and neighborhood, all these kinds of things, is not possible in China."—Text of a stock campaign speech from Bush's 1980 presidential bid[7]

"If we win in Michigan, it would be like a jockey or a marathon man with lead weights in both pockets. We've got the Anderson thing, and we've got this perception thing."—Speculating on his chances of winning the Michigan presidential primary in 1980. The "Anderson thing" refers to uncertainty over the popularity of maverick Republican presidential candidate John B. Anderson. The "perception thing" referred to the conventional wisdom that Ronald Reagan already had the nomination locked up[8]

"This idea that there's some kind of conspiracy [against] Mrs. Ferraro and the feminist thing is absolutely absurd."—When asked by a Detroit television station if he thought it was demeaning that his supporters had taken to using the term "kick ass" in reference to Bush's comment after his 1984 vice presidential debate with Geraldine Ferraro that he had tried to "kick a little ass."[9]

"And it didn't bother me when during the Vietnam war, much of the opposition of the government, Democrat and Republican governments, was led by priests, encouraging people to break the law and the adage of, you know, the civil disobedience thing."—During his 1984 vice presidential debate with Geraldine Ferraro[10]

". . . waving that thing in my face."—Bush's description of a confrontation with Senator Robert Dole on the Senate floor, in which Dole took offense at a statement released by the Bush campaign that accused him of "cronyism" and blamed him for Jimmy Carter's victory in 1976. Dole was the GOP vice presidential nominee in 1976. An irate Dole brought a copy of the statement to the Senate floor and confronted Bush with it[11]

"I have this horrible problem in figuring this thing out."—After losing a bid for a Texas Senate seat in 1970[12]

"I've got to figure out what I'm going to do. It's causing a firestorm, that thing."—Remarking on the public's outraged reaction to the proposed fifty-percent pay hike for top federal officials, including the President, the Vice President, and members of Congress[13]

FOOTNOTES

1. *Wall Street Journal,* Ellen Hume, August 15, 1988, p. 40

2. *Spy,* August 1988, p. 102

3. *In These Times,* Jeff Nason and Malcolm Byrne, February 16, 1988, p. 10

4. *Spy,* August 1988, p. 100

5. *Spy,* August 1988, p. 102

6. *New York Times,* January 5, 1980, p. B12

7. *New York Times,* March 2, 1980, p. D9

8. *New York Times,* May 19, 1980, p. B13

9. *Washington Post,* October 25, 1984, p. A7

10. *Washington Post,* October 12, 1984, p. A16

11. *Washington Post,* Ann Devoy, February 5, 1988, p. A11

12. *Washington Post,* Al Kamer with William F. Powers Jr., July 16, 1988, p. A4

13. *All Things Considered,* on National Public Radio, as quoted by Daniel Schorr, January 25, 1989

EIGHT

Some Reflections from Dan Quayle

"I'll be out at the appropriate time to make that announcement, and it will be laden with suspense . . . and everyone will say 'What a fantastic choice.'"—George Bush commenting on speculation over who he would choose as his running mate in 1988[1]

"Ladies and gentlemen, that big river [the Mississippi] had me thinking, and I've decided to share some big thoughts with you."—George Bush announcing his choice of Dan Quayle as his vice presidential running mate in 1988[2]

When George Bush announced that he had chosen Indiana Senator Dan Quayle to be his running mate, the question everyone asked was, "Why Quayle?" Immediately dubbed "Bush lite" by the press, the junior senator from Indiana, it turned out, had a less than sterling record.

It was alleged that Quayle had used family connections to get into the Indiana National Guard and avoid being sent to Vietnam, he had used a special program for disadvantaged students to get admitted to Indiana University Law School, and he steadfastly refused to release his college grades.

Before choosing Quayle as his running mate, Bush only did a superficial check of the senator's background. Bush was determined to make the selection of a running mate as dignified as possible, maybe because his own selection in 1980 was so awkward. At the 1980 convention Bush was largely perceived as a second choice, after a flurry of rumors that Gerald Ford would accept the second spot with Ronald Reagan on the GOP ticket.

Quayle immediately became a favorite of political satirists. Editorial cartoonists portrayed him as a ten-year-old boy in short pants, and motorists bought bumper stickers that said *Honk If You're Smarter Than Dan Quayle.*

Like all good political wives, Marilyn Quayle came to her husband's defense. She said the public should not make an issue out of Quayle's poor academic record. Later she described her husband as a "smart man" who "tries to read Plato's *Republic* every year."[3]

A former professor had a slightly different evaluation. "As vapid a student as I can recall," said Michael Lawrence, who taught Quayle at Depauw University[4]

But George stood by his choice. "He didn't go to Canada, he didn't burn his draft card, and he damn sure didn't burn the American flag," Bush said to a Veterans of Foreign Wars convention in Chicago[5]

Pundits said Bush chose the telegenic Quayle for his good looks, others said the hawkish forty-one-year-old was an appeal to conservative and younger voters, while Quayle himself ventured that he may have been chosen for his expertise on foreign affairs.

It appears, however, that there may have been a reason completely overlooked by the press and the pundits: Quayle shares Bush's wacky, if unintentional, sense of humor, and his arms-length relationship with the English language.

"The Holocaust was an obscene period in our nation's history. I mean this century's history. But we all lived in this century. I didn't live in this century."—Quayle discussing the Holocaust with reporters[6]

"I'll have to check with my dad."—Quayle's response when an Indiana GOP county chairman asked him to run for Congress in 1976[7]

"Verbosity leads to unclear, inarticulate things."—Explaining that he planned to be more careful with his words[8]

"The first would be our family. Your family, my family—which is composed of an immediate family of a wife and three children, a larger family with grandparents and aunts and uncles. We all have our family, whichever that may be."—Delivering a speech on the meaning of Thanksgiving in Charles City, Virginia[9]

"Republicans understand the importance of the bondage between parent and child."—At a GOP rally in September 1988, in Springfield, Illinois[10]

"Intrapersonal."—Describing his relationship with Bush on the campaign trail in Irvine, California[11]

He referred to ending the drug problem as a "nice idea."[12]

"I did not know in 1969 that I would be in this room today, I'll confess."—Responding to questions in 1988 about allegations that he used family connections to get into the Indiana National Guard[13]

"I deserve respect for the things I did not do."—Responding to questions about his admission to Indiana University Law School[14]

"I [did] what any normal person would do at that age. You call home. You call home to Mother and Father and say, 'I'd like to get into the National Guard.' "—Answering charges that he was a draft dodger during the Vietnam war[15]

Quayle had said his experience in the National Guard taught him many valuable skills, such as being able to weld. When visiting a welding class at a vocational school in Union, Missouri, he deftly welded two scraps of metal together to demonstrate. "That's solid. There, you see how much I learned."[16]

"When you get into conflict, and regional conflicts, I mean, you have to have certain goals, and a goal cannot be really a no-win situation."—Attempting to explain his military service during the Vietnam war[17]

"Bobby Knight [Indiana University basketball coach] told me this: 'There is nothing that a good defense cannot beat a better offense.' In other words, a good offense wins."—Garbling a quotation in a 1988 speech to the City Club of Chicago on nuclear weapons. Quayle left his audience confused about which strategy he preferred[18]

"Right now we have a theory of mutually assured destruction that supposedly provides for peace and stability, and it's worked. But that doesn't mean that we can't build upon a concept of MAD where both sides are vulnerable to another attack. Why wouldn't an enhanced deterrent, a more stable peace, a better prospect to denying the ones who enter conflict in the first place to have a reduction of offensive systems and an introduction to defensive capability. I believe that is the route this country will eventually go."—Discussing nuclear weapons at the same 1988 speech in Chicago[19]

"You can't just walk into a store and buy a gun. There's all sorts of registration, there are all sorts of state laws."—After criticizing Michael Dukakis for the Massachusetts furlough program, Quayle was informed that in many states a person could simply walk into a store and buy a gun.[20]

"It's rural America. It's where I came from. We always refer to ourselves as real America. Rural America, real America, real, real America."—Responding to questions about his statement that "rural Americans are real Americans"[21]

"Somewhere between real and real real."—Pinpointing their location to reporters aboard the Quayle campaign plane[22]

"I would just say a prayer and call a cabinet meeting."—When asked in the vice presidential debate what he would do if he had to assume the duties of the presidency[23]

Speaking to tired factory workers at the end of the day in Ohio, Quayle informed the workers that his children enjoyed playing lacrosse and soccer and riding horseback.[24]

"Life has been very good to me. I never had to worry about where I was going to go. But I do say, 'Dan, you know, sometime in life there's going to be a tragedy.' "—Self-reflection on the campaign trail in 1988[25]

"There was never anything where 'I've got to work really hard to get there . . .' "[26]

Quayle explained that the Democrats would lead this country "past backwards" if elected[27]

During a somewhat heated exchange with reporters in 1988, Quayle indicated he would only accept "yes or no" questions for the rest of the session. One reporter asked him if, in light of the controversy surrounding his stint in the National Guard, he had offered to take his name off the ticket. "That is not a yes or no question," Quayle responded.[28]

Bush described himself and Dan Quayle as "the pit bulls of American politics."[29]

"Let me say it one more time. It is ill-rel-e-vant."—Testily responding to repeated questions about his parents' involvement in the John Birch Society. When reporters asked him why it was irrelevant, he replied, "Because I said so."[30]

"And it was a very good book of Rasputin's involvement in that, which shows how people that are really very weird can get into sensitive positions and have a tremendous impact on history."—Dan Quayle giving his book report about *Nicholas and Alexandra* to Hendrick Hertzberg of the *New Republic.*[31]

"Another Jimmy Carter grain embargo, Jimmy Jimmy Carter, Jimmy Carter grain embargo, Jimmy Carter grain embargo."—Commenting on, you guessed it, the Jimmy Carter grain embargo, during his 1988 vice presidential debate with Lloyd Bentsen[32]

"I think, unfortunately, I had to be the target, that this bimbo thing was going to be applied to men someday, and I hate it. And I know what some of the unjustified charges of some women in the past have been, and I think it's rather despicable, and I think I'll outgrow it and get over it, but no, I don't like it one damn bit."— To National Public Radio's Nina Totenberg on the accusation that Quayle is stupid[33]

"One learns every day. Experience is a great teacher. By experience you learn. But as I enter office, I'm prepared now. Obviously, I will be more prepared as time goes on. I will know more about the office of the presidency. But I'm prepared now and I will be more prepared as time goes on."[34]

"They asked me to go in front of the Reagans. I'm not used to going in front of President Reagan, so we went out behind the Bushes."— After the swearing in ceremony on Inauguration Day, January 20, 1989[35]

FOOTNOTES

1. *Washington Post,* July 22, 1988, p. A28

2. *Washington Post,* August 17, 1988, p. A1

3. *New York Times,* Lisa Belkin, September 11, 1988, p. 32

4. *Washington Post,* August 23, 1988, p. A15

5. *Washington Post,* August 23, 1988, p. 1

6. *Spy,* November 1988, p. 128

7. *Washington Post,* October 2, 1988, p. 1

8. Associated Press, Washington, D.C., December 1, 1988

9. *Wall Street Journal,* Ronald Shafer, November 14, 1988, p. A9

10. *In These Times,* Maggie Garb, September 27, 1988, p. 5

11. *New York Times,* Maureen Dowd, August 28, 1988, p. 24

12. *Washington Post,* October 10, 1988, p. B10

13. *Washington Post,* Michael Isikoff and Joe Pichirallo, August 26, 1988, p. A6

14. *Manhattan Inc.,* John Seabrook, November 1988, p. 95

15. *Spy,* November 1988, p. 126

16. *New York Times,* Bernard Weinraub, October 25, 1988

17. *Washington Post,* Phillip Geyelin, September 6, 1988, p. A21

18. *New York Times,* Lisa Belkin, September 9, 1988, p. A14

19. Ibid

20. *New York Times,* Maureen Dowd, August 27, 1988, p. 6

21. *Wall Street Journal,* Michael McQueen, October 21, 1988

22. Ibid

23. *New York Times,* B. Drummond Ayres Jr., October 11, 1988

24. *Washington Post,* October 2, 1988, p. 1

25. *Washington Post,* October 10, 1988, p. B10

26. Ibid

27. *Washington Post,* Bill Peterson, August 18, 1988, p. A27

28. *Washington Post,* August 20, 1988, p. A6

29. Ibid

30. *Washington Post,* October 10, 1988, p. B10

31. *Savvy Woman,* January 1989, p. 56

32. *Spy,* February 1989, p. 80

33. Ibid

34. *New York Times,* January 14, 1989, p. 7

35. New York *Daily News,* Bill Bell, January 21, 1989, pp. 4, 5

THE AUTOBIOGRAPHY OF
ROY COHN

by Sidney Zion

"FASCINATING!"—*New York Post*

There were no neutrals in Roy Cohn's life.

His friends saw him as a patriot, a loyal pal, a fearless attorney and a party-thrower nonpareil.

His enemies knew him as a native fascist, Joe McCarthy's brains, and the legal executioner of Ethel and Julius Rosenberg.

Renowned journalist, lawyer and author, Sid Zion was a trusted friend of Cohn's for over 20 years. During the last years of his life, Cohn worked closely with Zion to fashion this book. The results are explosive.

With 8 pages of candid photos.

LANDMARK
BESTSELLERS
FROM ST. MARTIN'S PRESS